Morgan Donovan

How To Profit From Facebook

Your Ultimate Guide to Earning Income Online

Copyright © 2024 by Morgan Donovan

All rights reserved. No part of this publication may be reproduced, stored or transmitted in any form or by any means, electronic, mechanical, photocopying, recording, scanning, or otherwise without written permission from the publisher. It is illegal to copy this book, post it to a website, or distribute it by any other means without permission.

First edition

This book was professionally typeset on Reedsy
Find out more at reedsy.com

"Success in the digital age requires adaptability, creativity, and a willingness to embrace change."

- Morgan Donovan

Contents

Foreword 1
Preface 3
1. Understanding the Facebook Ecosystem 6
2. Setting Up Your Profile for Success 13
3. Crafting an Engaging Page 21
4. Building a Community with Groups 29
5. Content is King 38
6. Mastering Facebook Ads 46
7. Utilizing Facebook Insights 54
8. Leveraging Facebook Live 63
9. Engaging Your Audience 73
10. Storytelling with Facebook Stories 81
    1.
    2.
    3.
    4.
    5.
    6.
    7.
    8.

9.
10.
11.

Foreword

Foreword

In an age where social media platforms reign supreme, Facebook stands out as a titan among giants. With billions of users worldwide, it has revolutionized the way we connect, communicate, and consume content. But beyond its role as a social network, Facebook has emerged as a formidable force in the world of business and entrepreneurship.

As we navigate the ever-changing landscape of the digital economy, the ability to monetize our online presence has become increasingly valuable. In this regard, Facebook offers a wealth of opportunities for individuals and businesses to leverage its vast reach and robust features to generate income.

In "How To Profit from Facebook: Your Guide to Earning Income Online," Morgan Donovan provides a comprehensive roadmap for navigating the complexities of Facebook monetization. Drawing on years of experience and expertise, Donovan offers practical strategies, actionable insights, and invaluable advice for anyone looking to harness the earning potential of this platform.

From optimizing your profile and creating engaging content to mastering Facebook Ads and building a loyal community, Donovan covers every aspect of Facebook monetization with clarity and depth. Whether you're a seasoned entrepreneur or a budding influencer, this book equips you with the tools and knowledge needed to thrive in the digital marketplace.

As we embark on this journey together, let us embrace the opportunities that Facebook presents and strive to unlock our full potential in the online world.

Warm regards,

[Morgan   Donovan   ]

Preface

Preface

In today's digital age, Facebook has evolved far beyond a platform for social interaction; it has become a powerful tool for generating income and building sustainable online businesses. The sheer size of its user base, coupled with its diverse array of features, makes Facebook an unparalleled opportunity for entrepreneurs, influencers, and businesses alike.

When I first ventured into the realm of Facebook monetization, I was overwhelmed by the possibilities and the learning curve. Over time, through trial and error, diligent research, and a lot of persistence, I discovered strategies that transformed my social media presence into a significant income stream. These experiences fueled my passion for helping others navigate this dynamic landscape, leading to the creation of this book.

How To Profit from Facebook: Your Guide to Earning Income Online is designed to be your comprehensive guide to unlocking the financial potential of Facebook. Whether you are a small business owner looking to increase sales, an aspiring influencer eager to monetize your following, or simply someone interested in exploring new income avenues, this book provides the tools and insights you need to succeed.

Throughout these pages, you will find step-by-step strategies for leveraging Facebook's vast ecosystem. From mastering Facebook Ads and optimizing your business page to engaging your audience and creating compelling content, every chapter is packed with actionable advice and real-world examples. You will also discover how to harness the power of Facebook Groups, live videos, and Stories to build a loyal community and generate revenue.

My journey has shown me that success on Facebook isn't about overnight miracles or viral sensations. It's about understanding the platform's nuances, consistently delivering value to your audience, and adapting to the ever-changing digital environment. With this book, I aim to share not just the techniques but also the mindset needed to thrive.

I invite you to embark on this journey with me. Let's transform your Facebook presence into a lucrative venture and unlock the full potential of this incredible platform.

Welcome to the world of Facebook monetization.

Sincerely,

Morgan   Donovan

1

Understanding the Facebook Ecosystem

Understanding the Facebook Ecosystem

Introduction

Facebook has evolved from a simple social networking site to a complex ecosystem with a variety of features tailored for different purposes. Understanding these features is crucial to effectively using Facebook for personal branding, business marketing, or community building.

Profiles: Your Personal Hub
What is a Facebook Profile?

A Facebook profile is your personal hub on the platform, representing individual users. It includes personal information, photos, friends list, and your activity on the platform.

Key Features:

Timeline: A chronological feed of your posts, including status updates, photos, videos, and shared content.

About Section: Contains your personal information such as bio, work and education, contact info, and interests.

Friends: A list of your connections on Facebook. You can manage your friends, create friend lists, and control privacy settings for your posts.

Photos: Albums and individual photos you have uploaded, tagged in, or shared.

Best Practices:

Complete Your Profile: Fill out all relevant sections to make your profile more engaging and easier to find.

Privacy Settings: Regularly review and adjust your privacy settings to control who sees your information and posts.

Engage Regularly: Stay active by posting updates, engaging with friends' posts, and participating in conversations.

Pages: Building Your Brand
What is a Facebook Page?

A Facebook page is designed for businesses, brands, celebrities, and organizations to create a presence on Facebook. Unlike profiles, pages are public and can be liked and followed by anyone on Facebook.

Key Features:

Page Info: Includes details about your business or brand, such as address, hours of operation, and contact information.

Posts: Pages can share updates, photos, videos, events, and more to engage with their audience.

Insights: Access to analytics on page performance, audience demographics, and post engagement.

Call-to-Action Buttons: Customizable buttons on your page that drive specific actions like contacting you, booking appointments, or visiting your website.

Best Practices:

Optimize Your Page: Use a professional profile picture and cover photo, and ensure all information is complete and up-to-date.

Post Consistently: Regularly share high-quality content that resonates with your audience.

Engage with Followers: Respond to comments and messages promptly to build a loyal community.

Groups: Fostering Communities
What is a Facebook Group?

Facebook groups are communities where people with shared interests can connect, share content, and engage in discussions. Groups can be public, closed, or secret, providing various levels of privacy and access.

Key Features:

Discussion Threads: Members can start and participate in discussions on various topics.

Events: Groups can create events that members can join and participate in.

Files and Media Sharing: Members can share documents, photos, and videos within the group.

Group Rules: Admins can set rules and guidelines to ensure the group remains focused and respectful.

Best Practices:

Create Clear Guidelines: Establish and enforce group rules to maintain a positive and focused community.

Encourage Participation: Foster engagement by prompting discussions, sharing valuable content, and recognizing active members.

Monitor Activity: Regularly monitor group activity to ensure compliance with guidelines and address any issues promptly.

The News Feed: Your Information Stream

What is the News Feed?

The news feed is the central hub where users see a curated stream of updates from their friends, pages they follow, and groups they belong to. The content displayed in the news feed is determined by Facebook's algorithms, which prioritize posts based on user engagement, relevance, and recency.

Key Features:

Stories: Short, ephemeral content that disappears after 24 hours, appearing at the top of the news feed.

Sponsored Posts: Advertisements that appear within the news feed, targeting users based on their interests and behaviors.

Algorithmic Curation: Facebook uses algorithms to display content most relevant to each user, based on their interactions and preferences.

Best Practices:

Post Engaging Content: Create posts that encourage likes, comments, and shares to increase visibility.

Use Stories Effectively: Share behind-the-scenes content and timely updates through Facebook Stories to keep your audience engaged.

Monitor Insights: Regularly check your post performance and adjust your content strategy accordingly.

Conclusion

Understanding the Facebook ecosystem is the first step toward leveraging the platform for your success. By effectively using profiles, pages, groups, and the news feed, you can create a robust presence on Facebook that attracts and engages your desired audience.

2

Setting Up Your Profile for Success

Setting Up Your Profile for Success

Creating a compelling Facebook profile is essential for attracting the right audience, whether you're aiming for personal connections or business networking. A well-crafted profile showcases your personality or brand and makes a strong first impression.

Step 1: Choose the Right Profile Picture

Why It Matters:

Your profile picture is the first thing people see. It should be clear, professional, and representative of you or your brand.

Tips:

For Personal Profiles: Use a high-quality photo of yourself, preferably a headshot with good lighting and a neutral background.

For Business Profiles: Use your business logo or a professional image that represents your brand.

Step 2: Craft an Engaging Cover Photo

Why It Matters:

The cover photo is a large banner image at the top of your profile. It provides an opportunity to showcase more about you or your brand.

Tips:

For Personal Profiles: Use a photo that reflects your interests or passions, such as a landscape, a hobby, or a special event.

For Business Profiles: Use a branded image that highlights your products, services, or a significant aspect of your business.

Step 3: Fill Out the About Section

Why It Matters:

The About section provides detailed information about you or your business, helping others understand who you are and what you offer.

Tips:

Personal Profiles: Include your bio, work and education history, contact information, and interests. Keep it concise and engaging.

Business Profiles: Provide a clear and detailed description of your business, including your mission, services, location, and contact details.

Step 4: Customize Your URL

Why It Matters:

A custom URL makes it easier for people to find and remember your profile.

Tips:

Go to the settings and create a custom username that aligns with your name or brand. For example, facebook.com/YourName or facebook.com/YourBusinessName.

Step 5: Add Key Milestones and Highlights

Why It Matters:

Highlighting significant events and milestones gives your profile a narrative and shows your journey.

Tips:

Personal Profiles: Add important life events such as graduation, new job, or major achievements.

Business Profiles: Highlight key moments like your business launch, major product releases, awards, or other notable events.

Step 6: Share High-Quality Content

Why It Matters:

Regularly sharing valuable content keeps your profile active and engaging.

Tips:

Personal Profiles: Share posts that reflect your interests, insights, and experiences. Use photos, videos, and links to enhance your posts.

Business Profiles: Post a mix of content including product updates, industry news, behind-the-scenes looks, customer testimonials, and promotions.

Step 7: Engage with Your Audience

Why It Matters:

Interaction fosters relationships and builds a community around your profile.

Tips:

Personal Profiles: Comment on friends' posts, join relevant groups, and participate in discussions.

Business Profiles: Respond promptly to comments and messages, ask questions to encourage engagement, and acknowledge your followers' contributions.

Step 8: Utilize Facebook Stories

Why It Matters:

Facebook Stories are a great way to share short, engaging content that captures immediate interest.

Tips:

Personal Profiles: Use Stories to share daily moments, updates, and quick tips.

Business Profiles: Use Stories to showcase new products, share quick tutorials, offer behind-the-scenes looks, and run time-sensitive promotions.

Step 9: Optimize Your Privacy Settings

Why It Matters:

Controlling who sees your information and posts ensures your profile is safe and professional.

Tips:

Review your privacy settings regularly.

Choose who can see your posts, send you friend requests, and find you via search engines.

Customize the audience for each post if needed.

Step 10: Keep Your Profile Updated

Why It Matters:

An up-to-date profile ensures that all information is current and accurate, which builds trust and relevance.

Tips: Regularly review and update your profile picture, cover photo, and About section.

Add new milestones, achievements, and relevant content as they happen.

Conclusion

Setting up a compelling Facebook profile is about presenting yourself or your brand in the best light possible. By following these steps, you can create a profile that attracts the right audience, engages visitors, and sets a strong foundation for your Facebook success.

3

Crafting an Engaging Page

Crafting an Engaging Page

Creating a standout Facebook page is crucial for personal branding or business marketing. Your page serves as the face of your brand on Facebook, and it's where you engage with your audience, share updates, and build a community.

Step 1: Set Up Your Page

Why It Matters:

The setup is the foundation of your page. A well-set-up page looks professional and is easy for users to navigate.

Tips: Go to the Facebook homepage and click on "Create" in the top right corner.

Select "Page" from the drop-down menu.

Choose "Business or Brand" or "Community or Public Figure" depending on your goal.

Enter your page name and category (e.g., local business, personal blog, etc.).

Step 2: Add Profile and Cover Photos

Why It Matters:

Visuals are the first impression visitors get. High-quality images make your page look professional and attractive.

Tips:

Profile Photo: Use your logo or a professional image that represents your brand.

Cover Photo: Choose a high-quality image that reflects your brand's identity or key messages. Ensure it's properly sized (820x312 pixels for desktop, 640x360 pixels for mobile).

Step 3: Complete the About Section

Why It Matters:

The About section provides crucial information about your page, helping visitors understand who you are and what you offer.

Tips:

Page Info: Fill in all relevant details, including a brief description, contact information, website, and hours of operation.

Additional Information: Add a mission statement, company overview, and other pertinent information.

Step 4: Create a Username

Why It Matters:

A custom username makes your page easier to find and promotes consistency across social media platforms.

Tips:

Go to your page and click on "Create @Username" under your page name.

Choose a username that's simple, memorable, and reflective of your brand.

Step 5: Add a Call-to-Action Button

Why It Matters:

A call-to-action (CTA) button encourages visitors to take specific actions, such as contacting you or visiting your website.

Tips:

Click on the "Add a Button" option below your cover photo.

Choose the most relevant CTA for your goals, such as "Contact Us," "Shop Now," or "Learn More."

Link it to the appropriate destination, like your website or contact form.

Step 6: Optimize Page Tabs

Why It Matters:

Page tabs help organize your content and make it easy for visitors to find what they're looking for.

Tips:

Go to "Settings" > "Templates and Tabs."

Customize the tabs according to your needs, such as Videos, Events, Offers, Services, etc.

Arrange the tabs in an order that prioritizes your most important content.

Step 7: Post High-Quality Content

Why It Matters:

Regularly posting engaging content keeps your audience interested and coming back for more.

Tips:

Content Mix: Share a variety of content types, including articles, videos, photos, and links.

Quality Over Quantity: Focus on creating high-quality posts that provide value to your audience.

Consistency: Develop a posting schedule to keep your page active and engaging.

Step 8: Engage with Your Audience

Why It Matters:

Active engagement builds a loyal community and fosters strong relationships with your followers.

Tips:

Respond Promptly: Reply to comments and messages in a timely manner.

Ask Questions: Encourage interaction by asking questions and prompting discussions.

Show Appreciation: Acknowledge your followers' contributions and thank them for their support.

Step 9: Use Facebook Insights

Why It Matters:

Facebook Insights provide valuable data on your page's performance, helping you understand what works and what doesn't.

Tips:

Access Insights from the top menu of your page.

Monitor key metrics such as page views, likes, reach, and engagement.

Use this data to refine your content strategy and improve your page's performance.

Step 10: Promote Your Page

Why It Matters:

Promotion helps you reach a wider audience and grow your follower base.

Tips:

Invite Friends: Start by inviting your friends to like your page.

Share Your Page: Post about your new page on your personal profile and other social media platforms.

Facebook Ads: Consider running Facebook ads to target specific audiences and boost your page's visibility.

Conclusion

Crafting an engaging Facebook page involves careful planning and consistent effort. By following these steps, you can create a page that not only stands out but also serves your goals effectively.

4

Building a Community with Groups

Building a Community with Groups

Facebook groups are powerful tools for creating communities around your brand or interests. They offer a space for deeper engagement, discussions, and connections among members.

Step 1: Define Your Group's Purpose

Why It Matters:

A clear purpose attracts the right members and sets the tone for your group's activities and discussions.

Tips:

Identify the primary goal of your group. Is it to support customers, share knowledge, build a network, or discuss specific topics?

Write a concise mission statement to clearly communicate the group's purpose.

Step 2: Create Your Group

Why It Matters:

Setting up your group correctly from the start ensures it aligns with your objectives and is easily discoverable by potential members.

Tips:

Go to the Facebook homepage, click on "Create" and select "Group."

Enter your group name. Choose something descriptive and easy to remember.

Select the privacy setting: Public, Closed, or Secret. Closed groups are often best for fostering a sense of community while maintaining some level of privacy.

Invite initial members from your network to kickstart engagement.

Step 3: Set Up Group Details

Why It Matters:

Detailed group information helps potential members understand what the group is about and encourages them to join.

Tips:

Description: Write a detailed description that includes the group's purpose, rules, and what members can expect.

Tags: Add relevant tags to improve your group's visibility in search results.

Cover Photo: Upload a high-quality cover photo that represents the group's theme or purpose.

Step 4: Establish Group Rules

Why It Matters:

Clear rules help maintain a positive and respectful environment, preventing conflicts and misunderstandings.

Tips:

Outline the dos and don'ts in your group description or create a dedicated post.

Enforce rules consistently and fairly to maintain group harmony.

Pin the rules post to the top of the group to ensure all members see it.

Step 5: Create Engaging Content

Why It Matters:

Regular and engaging content keeps the group active and members interested.

Tips:

Discussion Posts: Ask open-ended questions to spark discussions.

Polls and Surveys: Use polls to gather opinions and feedback from members.

Multimedia Content: Share photos, videos, and live streams to make content more engaging.

Exclusive Content: Offer special content like tutorials, articles, or insider news that's only available to group members.

Step 6: Foster Member Engagement

Why It Matters:

Engagement is the lifeblood of any community. Active members are more likely to contribute, stay longer, and invite others.

Tips:

Welcome New Members: Post a welcome message for new members and encourage them to introduce themselves.

Highlight Contributions: Recognize and appreciate active members by highlighting their contributions.

Host Events: Organize virtual events, such as Q&A sessions, webinars, or live chats to bring members together.

Step 7: Moderate Effectively

Why It Matters:

Effective moderation ensures the group remains focused, respectful, and valuable to all members.

Tips:

Appoint Moderators: If your group grows large, appoint trusted members as moderators to help manage posts and enforce rules.

Review Posts: Depending on your group's settings, you might need to approve posts before they go live to maintain quality.

Address Issues Promptly: Handle conflicts, spam, and rule violations quickly to maintain a positive environment.

Step 8: Grow Your Group

Why It Matters:

A growing group means more diverse discussions and a broader reach for your brand or interest.

Tips:

Promote Your Group: Share your group on your Facebook page, profile, other social media platforms, and your website.

Collaborate with Influencers: Partner with influencers in your niche to promote the group.

Encourage Member Invitations: Motivate current members to invite friends who might be interested.

Step 9: Analyze and Adapt

Why It Matters:

Regular analysis helps you understand what's working and what needs improvement to keep the group thriving.

Tips:

Monitor Engagement: Use Facebook's group insights to track member activity, engagement rates, and growth.

Gather Feedback: Periodically ask members for feedback on how to improve the group.

Adapt Strategies: Based on insights and feedback, adjust your content, engagement tactics, and group rules as needed.

Step 10: Keep the Community Spirit Alive

Why It Matters:

A strong community spirit keeps members connected and committed to the group.

Tips:

Be Present: Regularly participate in discussions and engage with members.

Celebrate Milestones: Celebrate group milestones such as member count achievements, anniversaries, or successful events.

Show Appreciation: Regularly thank members for their contributions and support.

Conclusion

Building a community with Facebook groups requires dedication and strategic planning. By following these steps, you can create a thriving group that fosters meaningful connections and engagement around your brand or interests.

5

Content is King

Content is King:

Developing a Content Strategy

Creating high-quality, engaging content is crucial for keeping your audience interested and coming back for more. A well-crafted content strategy helps you deliver consistent value, build trust, and foster a loyal community.

Step 1: Understand Your Audience

Why It Matters:

Knowing your audience's interests, preferences, and pain points helps you create content that truly resonates with them.

Tips:

Demographics: Use Facebook Insights to gather data on your audience's age, gender, location, and interests.

Surveys and Polls: Conduct surveys or polls to directly ask your audience what they want to see more of.

Engagement Analysis: Review which types of content have previously received the most engagement.

Step 2: Set Clear Goals

Why It Matters:

Clear goals give direction to your content strategy and help measure its success.

Tips:

Specific: Define specific goals such as increasing engagement, driving traffic to your website, or growing your follower base.

Measurable: Set measurable targets like a certain number of likes, shares, comments, or website visits.

Achievable: Ensure your goals are realistic and attainable given your resources and audience size.

Relevant: Align your goals with your overall brand or business objectives.

Time-bound: Set a timeline for achieving your goals, such as within three or six months.

Step 3: Develop Content Themes and Pillars

Why It Matters:

Content themes and pillars provide a structured framework for your content, ensuring consistency and variety.

Tips:

Identify Key Themes: Determine broad topics that are relevant to your brand and audience. These could include industry news, how-to guides, behind-the-scenes looks, customer stories, etc.

Content Pillars: Break down each theme into specific content ideas. For example, if one of your themes is "Product Tips," content pillars could include tutorials, FAQs, and customer success stories.

Step 4: Create a Content Calendar

Why It Matters:

A content calendar helps you plan, organize, and schedule your content, ensuring a consistent posting frequency.

Tips:

Monthly Planning: Plan your content a month in advance to maintain a steady flow of posts.

Include Key Dates: Mark important dates, such as holidays, events, or product launches, to align your content accordingly.

Variety of Formats: Schedule a mix of content formats, including text posts, images, videos, and live sessions.

Step 5: Craft High-Quality Content

Why It Matters:

High-quality content attracts attention, drives engagement, and builds credibility.

Tips:

Clear and Concise: Write clear, concise, and compelling posts. Avoid jargon and keep the language simple.

Visual Appeal: Use high-quality images, graphics, and videos to make your content visually appealing.

Value-Driven: Focus on providing value to your audience, whether through education, entertainment, or inspiration.

Storytelling: Use storytelling techniques to make your content more engaging and relatable.

Step 6: Optimize for Engagement

Why It Matters:

Optimizing your content for engagement increases the likelihood of likes, shares, comments, and interactions.

Tips:

Call to Action: Include clear calls to action in your posts, encouraging your audience to like, share, comment, or visit your website.

Questions and Polls: Ask questions or create polls to prompt audience interaction.

Timing: Post when your audience is most active. Use Facebook Insights to determine the best times to post.

Tagging and Hashtags: Tag relevant pages, people, and use hashtags to increase your content's reach.

Step 7: Leverage User-Generated Content

Why It Matters:

User-generated content (UGC) builds community, fosters trust, and provides fresh content for your page.

Tips:

Encourage Sharing: Ask your audience to share their experiences, photos, or stories related to your brand.

Feature UGC: Regularly feature user-generated content on your page, giving credit to the original creators.

Contests and Challenges: Run contests or challenges that prompt your audience to create and share content.

Step 8: Analyze and Adjust

Why It Matters:

Regular analysis helps you understand what's working and what needs improvement, allowing you to refine your strategy.

Tips:

Track Metrics: Monitor key metrics such as reach, engagement, clicks, and shares using Facebook Insights.

Content Performance: Identify which types of content perform best and why.

Feedback Loop: Collect feedback from your audience to understand their preferences and make adjustments accordingly.

Continuous Improvement: Use the insights gained to continuously improve and adapt your content strategy.

Conclusion

Developing a content strategy that resonates with your audience is key to building a loyal and engaged community on Facebook. By understanding your audience, setting clear goals, planning your content, and regularly analyzing performance, you can create high-quality content that keeps your followers coming back for more.

6

Mastering Facebook Ads

Mastering Facebook Ads

Facebook advertising is a powerful tool that can significantly amplify your reach and impact.

Step 1: Understanding Facebook Ads

Why It Matters:

Knowing the basics of Facebook ads helps you leverage the platform's powerful targeting and engagement tools to reach your desired audience effectively.

Types of Facebook Ads:

Image Ads: Simple ads featuring a single image.

Video Ads: Ads featuring a video, which can be more engaging than static images.

Carousel Ads: Ads that showcase multiple images or videos that users can swipe through.

Collection Ads: Ads that allow users to browse products directly from the ad.

Slideshow Ads: Lightweight video ads made from a series of still images.

Instant Experience (Canvas) Ads: Full-screen ads that load instantly and offer a highly immersive experience.

Lead Generation Ads: Ads designed to capture leads directly within Facebook.

Step 2: Setting Up Your Facebook Ad Account

Why It Matters:

Before creating ads, you need to set up your Facebook Ad Account, which will manage your billing information and ad campaigns.

Tips:

Go to the Facebook Ads Manager.

Click on "Account Settings" to enter your business information.

Add your payment method to handle ad costs.

Step 3: Defining Your Campaign Objectives

Why It Matters:

Clear objectives guide your ad strategy and help measure the success of your campaigns.

Tips:

Awareness: Increase brand awareness or reach as many people as possible.

Consideration: Drive traffic, engagement, app installs, video views, lead generation, or messages.

Conversion: Encourage actions such as purchases, sign-ups, or visiting your store.

Step 4: Creating Your First Ad Campaign

Why It Matters:

A well-structured ad campaign can effectively reach and engage your target audience.

Tips:

1. Choose Your Objective:

Go to Ads Manager and click on "Create."

Select the campaign objective that aligns with your goals (e.g., Traffic, Engagement, Conversions).

2. Set Your Campaign Name:

Give your campaign a clear and descriptive name to keep your campaigns organized.

3. Define Your Audience:

Use Facebook's targeting options to define your audience based on location, age, gender, interests, and behaviors.

Consider creating custom audiences based on your existing customer data or lookalike audiences to find similar users.

4. Set Your Budget and Schedule:

Choose between a daily budget or a lifetime budget.

Set the start and end dates for your campaign or opt to run it continuously.

5. Choose Your Ad Placement:

Decide where your ads will appear (e.g., Facebook News Feed, Instagram, Messenger, Audience Network).

You can allow Facebook to automatically place your ads where they are likely to perform best.

6. Create Your Ad:

Choose the ad format (e.g., image, video, carousel).

Upload your media and write compelling ad copy.

Include a clear call-to-action (CTA) that aligns with your campaign objective.

Step 5: Monitoring and Optimizing Your Ads

Why It Matters:

Regularly monitoring and optimizing your ads ensures they perform well and provide a good return on investment.

Tips:

Track Performance: Use Ads Manager to monitor key metrics such as reach, impressions, clicks, and conversions.

A/B Testing: Run A/B tests to compare different versions of your ads and see which performs better.

Adjust Targeting: Refine your audience targeting based on performance data.

Optimize Budget: Allocate more budget to high-performing ads and pause or stop underperforming ones.

Step 6: Understanding Ad Analytics

Why It Matters:

Understanding ad analytics helps you make data-driven decisions to improve your campaigns.

Key Metrics to Monitor:

Reach: The number of unique users who saw your ad.

Impressions: The total number of times your ad was displayed.

Click-Through Rate (CTR): The percentage of people who clicked on your ad after seeing it.

Cost Per Click (CPC): The average cost of each click on your ad.

Conversion Rate: The percentage of users who completed a desired action after clicking on your ad.

Return on Ad Spend (ROAS): The revenue generated for every dollar spent on ads.

Step 7: Refining Your Strategy

Why It Matters:

Continuous improvement of your ad strategy ensures better results over time.

Tips:

Analyze Results: Regularly review your ad performance and identify trends.

Iterate: Make incremental changes based on insights gained from your analytics.

Stay Updated: Keep up with the latest Facebook ad features and best practices to stay ahead.

Conclusion

Mastering Facebook ads involves understanding the basics, setting up well-defined campaigns, monitoring performance, and continually optimizing your strategy. By following these steps, you can effectively leverage Facebook advertising to reach your target audience and achieve your marketing goals.

7

Utilizing Facebook Insights

Utilizing Facebook Insights

Facebook Insights is a powerful tool that provides detailed analytics about your page's performance and audience. Understanding how to use this data can help you refine your strategy, improve engagement, and achieve your goals more effectively.

Step 1: Accessing Facebook Insights

Why It Matters:

Accessing Insights is the first step to understanding your page's performance and audience behavior.

Tips:

Go to your Facebook page.

Click on "Insights" in the top menu to access the analytics dashboard.

Step 2: Overview of Key Metrics

Why It Matters:

Familiarizing yourself with key metrics helps you monitor your page's performance and identify areas for improvement.

Key Metrics:

Page Views: The number of times your page was viewed.

Page Likes: The total number of likes on your page.

Post Reach: The number of unique users who saw your posts.

Post Engagements: The number of interactions (likes, comments, shares) with your posts.

Page Followers: The number of people following your page.

Step 3: Analyzing Your Audience

Why It Matters:

Understanding your audience demographics and behaviors allows you to tailor your content and strategy to better meet their needs.

Tips:

Demographics: Check the "People" section to view age, gender, and location data of your followers.

Page Followers: Analyze the number of followers gained or lost over time to understand growth trends.

Audience Interests: Use insights to identify what content resonates most with your audience.

Step 4: Monitoring Post Performance

Why It Matters:

Analyzing individual post performance helps you identify what types of content are most effective.

Tips:

Post Reach:.Monitor how many people saw each post.

Engagement Rate: Track likes, comments, shares, and clicks to gauge engagement levels.

Best Times to Post: Identify when your audience is most active to optimize posting times.

Content Types: Compare the performance of different content types (e.g., photos, videos, links) to see what works best.

Step 5: Understanding Reach and Impressions

Why It Matters:Reach and impressions are key indicators of how widely your content is being viewed.

Tips:

Total Reach: Look at the number of unique users who saw your content.

Post Reach: Analyze the reach of individual posts to see which ones performed best.

Impressions: Track the total number of times your content was displayed, including multiple views by the same user.

Step 6: Tracking Engagement Metrics

Why It Matters: Engagement metrics provide insights into how your audience interacts with your content.

Tips:

Engagement Rate: Calculate the engagement rate by dividing the total engagements by the total reach.

Likes, Comments, Shares: Monitor these interactions to understand what content sparks conversation and sharing.

Click-Through Rate (CTR): Track how often people click on links in your posts.

Step 7: Using Insights to Refine Your Strategy

Why It Matters:

Regularly reviewing and analyzing insights allows you to make data-driven decisions and continuously improve your strategy.

Tips:

Content Optimization: Use insights to identify high-performing content and create more of what your audience likes.

Audience Targeting: Adjust your targeting based on demographic data and engagement trends.

Post Scheduling: Optimize posting times based on when your audience is most active.

Engagement Strategies: Develop strategies to boost engagement, such as asking questions, running polls, or creating interactive content.

Step 8: Monitoring Competitors

Why It Matters:

Keeping an eye on your competitors can provide valuable insights and inspiration for your own strategy.

Tips:

Pages to Watch: Use the "Pages to Watch" feature in Insights to track and compare the performance of similar pages.

Benchmarking: Compare your metrics against competitors to see how you stack up and identify areas for improvement.

Step 9: Customizing Reports

Why It Matters:

Customized reports allow you to focus on the metrics that matter most to your specific goals.

Tips:

Export Data: Export data from Insights to analyze it in more detail or share with your team.

Custom Date Ranges: Select specific date ranges to analyze performance over different periods.

Focus Areas: Customize reports to highlight key metrics and insights relevant to your goals.

Step 10: Staying Updated

Why It Matters:

Facebook regularly updates its features and analytics tools, so staying informed ensures you're making the most of the platform.

Tips:

Follow Updates: Keep an eye on Facebook's official announcements for new features and updates.

Continuous Learning: Participate in webinars, read blogs, and take online courses to stay current with best practices and new tools.

Experimentation: Regularly test new strategies and features to see what works best for your audience.

Conclusion

Utilizing Facebook Insights is essential for tracking performance, understanding your audience, and refining your strategy. By regularly analyzing your metrics, you can make informed decisions that enhance your content, increase engagement, and achieve your goals.

8

Leveraging Facebook Live

Leveraging Facebook Live

Facebook Live is a powerful tool that allows you to engage with your audience in real-time, providing an authentic and interactive way to boost visibility and foster community.

Step 1: Understanding the Benefits of Facebook Live

Why It Matters:

Knowing the benefits helps you harness the full potential of Facebook Live to engage with your audience.

Key Benefits:

Real-Time Interaction: Engage with your audience in real-time through comments and reactions.

Increased Visibility: Live videos often appear higher in the news feed, increasing reach.

Authenticity: Live streams provide a raw, unedited view that can build trust and authenticity.

Notifications: Followers receive notifications when you go live, driving immediate engagement.

Step 2: Planning Your Live Broadcast

Why It Matters:

Proper planning ensures your live session runs smoothly and achieves its objectives.

Tips:

Define Your Purpose: Determine the goal of your live session (e.g., Q&A, product demonstration, event coverage).

Outline Key Points: Plan the structure of your broadcast, including key topics and segments.

Choose a Time: Schedule your live session when your audience is most active. Use Facebook Insights to determine the best times.

Promote in Advance: Announce your live session ahead of time through posts, stories, and events to build anticipation.

Step 3: Setting Up for a Successful Broadcast

Why It Matters:

Proper setup enhances the quality and professionalism of your live broadcast.

Tips:

Stable Internet Connection: Ensure you have a strong and stable internet connection to avoid interruptions.

Lighting and Sound: Use good lighting and ensure your microphone captures clear audio.

Location: Choose a quiet, well-lit location free from distractions.

Equipment: Use a tripod for stability and consider external microphones and lighting for better quality.

Step 4: Going Live

Why It Matters:

Starting your broadcast correctly sets the tone for the session and engages viewers from the beginning.

Steps to Go Live:

1. Open Facebook: Navigate to your page or profile.

2. Start a Live Video: Click on "Live Video" from the post creation area.

3. Set Up Your Stream: Add a title and description to let viewers know what to expect.

4. Engage Immediately: Greet viewers as they join and introduce the topic. Encourage them to interact by commenting and reacting.

Step 5: Engaging with Your Audience

Why It Matters:

Active engagement keeps viewers interested and encourages interaction.

Tips:

Acknowledge Comments: Read and respond to comments and questions in real-time.

Ask Questions: Encourage viewers to participate by asking questions and inviting their input.

Shout-Outs: Give shout-outs to viewers by name to make them feel special and appreciated.

Use Reactions: Ask viewers to use reactions (likes, loves, etc.) to gauge their interest and feedback.

Step 6: Adding Interactive Elements

Why It Matters:

Interactive elements make your broadcast more engaging and dynamic.

Tips:

Polls and Q&A: Use Facebook's built-in features to create polls or host a Q&A session.

Guest Appearances: Invite guests to join your live session for interviews or discussions.

Screen Sharing: Share your screen to demonstrate products, showcase presentations, or review documents.

Step 7: Concluding Your Broadcast

Why It Matters:

Ending your broadcast effectively leaves a positive impression and encourages future engagement.

Tips:

Summarize Key Points: Recap the main takeaways of your live session.

Call to Action: Encourage viewers to take a specific action, such as visiting your website, signing up for a newsletter, or joining your group.

Thank Viewers: Express gratitude to your viewers for their participation and support.

End Smoothly: Click "Finish" to end your live session, and then save the video for future reference.

Step 8: Analyzing Your Live Video Performance

Why It Matters:

Analyzing performance helps you understand what worked well and identify areas for improvement.

Tips:

View Metrics: Check metrics such as total views, peak concurrent viewers, and average watch time.

Engagement Data: Analyze the number of comments, shares, reactions, and viewer demographics.

Feedback: Review comments and messages for feedback and suggestions from your audience.

Step 9: Repurposing Your Live Content

Why It Matters:

Repurposing extends the life of your content and reaches a broader audience.

Tips:

Save and Share: Save the live video and share it on your page, website, and other social media platforms.

Highlights: Create highlight clips of the most engaging parts of your broadcast.

Blog Posts: Write blog posts summarizing the key points discussed during your live session.

Email Newsletters: Include links to your live video in your email newsletters to reach subscribers.

Step 10: Continuous Improvement

Why It Matters:

Continual refinement ensures your live broadcasts remain engaging and effective.

Tips:

Review Analytics: Regularly review performance data and adjust your strategy accordingly.

Experiment: Try different formats, topics, and times to see what resonates best with your audience.

Solicit Feedback: Ask your audience for feedback on how to improve future live sessions.

Conclusion

Leveraging Facebook Live effectively can significantly boost your visibility, engage your audience in real-time, and foster a sense of community. By planning carefully, engaging actively, and continuously refining your approach, you can make the most of this dynamic platform.

9

Engaging Your Audience

Engaging Your Audience

Engaging with your audience is crucial for building a loyal and active community on Facebook. Effective interaction fosters trust, encourages participation, and enhances your brand's reputation.

Step 1: Responding to Comments

Why It Matters:

Responding to comments shows that you value your audience's input and fosters a sense of community.

Tips:

Be Prompt: Respond to comments as quickly as possible to keep the conversation alive.

Be Personal: Address commenters by their names and provide personalized responses.

Be Positive: Maintain a positive and friendly tone, even when addressing negative comments.

Acknowledge All Comments: Respond to both positive and negative comments to show that all feedback is valued.

Step 2: Managing Messages

Why It Matters: Handling messages effectively ensures that your audience feels heard and valued, and it can also help in resolving issues quickly.

Tips:

Enable Messaging: Ensure your page settings allow followers to send messages.

Use Instant Replies: Set up instant replies to acknowledge receipt of messages and let senders know when they can expect a response.

Personalize Responses: Tailor your responses to each individual, addressing their specific queries or concerns.

Be Timely: Aim to respond to messages within 24 hours to show that you value your audience's time and input.

Utilize Messenger Bots: For common inquiries, set up automated responses using Messenger bots to provide instant answers and guide users.

Step 3: Crafting Engaging Posts

Why It Matters: Engaging posts attract attention, provoke discussion, and encourage sharing, thereby increasing your reach and visibility.

Tips:

Ask Questions: Pose questions to your audience to prompt interaction and gather insights.

Use Visuals: Include high-quality images, graphics, and videos to make your posts more appealing.

Share Stories: Share stories and experiences that resonate with your audience on a personal level.

Offer Value: Provide valuable content such as tips, tutorials, and industry news.

Call to Action: Include clear calls to action, encouraging your audience to like, share, comment, or visit your website.

Step 4: Hosting Interactive Sessions

Why It Matters: Interactive sessions, like Q&A sessions or live polls, boost engagement and provide immediate feedback from your audience.

Tips:

Live Q&A: Host live Q&A sessions where you answer audience questions in real-time.

Polls and Surveys: Use polls and surveys to engage your audience and gather their opinions.

Contests and Giveaways: Run contests and giveaways to increase participation and excitement.

Interactive Stories: Use Facebook Stories to create interactive content like quizzes and behind-the-scenes looks.

Step 5: Creating a Sense of Community

Why It Matters: A strong sense of community encourages loyalty and active participation from your audience.

Tips:

Community Guidelines: Establish clear community guidelines to foster a positive and respectful environment.

Highlight Members: Regularly feature community members and their contributions.

Encourage User-Generated Content: Ask your audience to share their own content related to your brand.

Host Events: Organize both online and offline events to bring your community together.

Step 6: Monitoring Engagement Metrics

Why It Matters: Monitoring engagement metrics helps you understand what works and what doesn't, allowing you to refine your strategy.

Tips:

Track Key Metrics: Monitor likes, comments, shares, and reactions to gauge engagement levels.

Analyze Content Performance: Review which types of posts generate the most engagement.

Adjust Strategy: Use insights from engagement metrics to adjust your content and interaction strategies.

Step 7: Handling Negative Feedback

Why It Matters:

Addressing negative feedback constructively can turn a potentially damaging situation into a positive experience.

Tips:

Stay Calm: Keep your responses calm and professional, even in the face of criticism.

Acknowledge Concerns: Acknowledge the feedback and show that you take it seriously.

Offer Solutions: Provide solutions or direct the person to where they can get help.

Follow Up: Follow up to ensure the issue has been resolved and the person is satisfied.

Step 8: Encouraging Feedback and Suggestions

Why It Matters: Encouraging feedback helps you improve your content and services while making your audience feel valued.

Tips:

Ask for Feedback: Regularly ask your audience for their opinions and suggestions.

Create Feedback Channels: Provide easy ways for your audience to give feedback, such as surveys or feedback forms.

Act on Feedback: Show that you value feedback by implementing suggestions and acknowledging contributions.

Conclusion

Engaging your audience through comments, messages, and posts is essential for building a loyal and active community on Facebook. By responding promptly, creating engaging content, hosting interactive sessions, and fostering a sense of community, you can strengthen your relationship with your audience and enhance your brand's reputation.

10

Storytelling with Facebook Stories

Storytelling with Facebook Stories

Facebook Stories offer a unique way to connect with your audience by sharing authentic, behind-the-scenes content. This ephemeral format allows you to tell stories that disappear after 24 hours, creating a sense of urgency and exclusivity.

Step 1: Understanding the Power of Facebook Stories

Why It Matters:

Facebook Stories provide a more casual and immediate way to connect with your audience, fostering a sense of intimacy and authenticity.

Key Benefits:

Ephemeral Content: Stories disappear after 24 hours, encouraging timely engagement.

Visibility: Stories appear at the top of the news feed, ensuring they are prominently displayed.

Engagement: Interactive features like polls, questions, and stickers boost audience interaction.

Behind-the-Scenes Access: Stories offer a glimpse into your brand's daily life, making your content more relatable.

Step 2: Creating Compelling Stories

Why It Matters: Engaging and well-crafted stories keep your audience interested and encourage them to return for more.

Tips:

Be Authentic: Share real moments and behind-the-scenes content to build trust.

Be Consistent: Post regularly to keep your audience engaged and looking forward to your stories.

Use Variety: Mix different content types, such as photos, videos, boomerangs, and text.

Keep It Short: Each story should be concise and to the point to maintain viewer interest.

Example:

Share a short video of your team preparing for an upcoming event, highlighting the excitement and effort that goes into it.

Step 3: Utilizing Interactive Features

Why It Matters:

Interactive elements increase engagement and make your stories more dynamic and interesting.

Tips:

Polls: Use polls to gather opinions and feedback from your audience.

Questions: Invite your audience to ask questions or share their thoughts.

Stickers: Add location tags, hashtags, and stickers to make your stories more engaging.

Links: If you have a verified account or more than 10,000 followers, use the swipe-up feature to direct viewers to your website or other content.

Example:

Run a poll asking your audience to choose between two new product designs, and share the results in a follow-up story.

Step 4: Telling a Story with Multiple Frames

Why It Matters:

Using multiple frames allows you to create a narrative and keep your audience engaged from start to finish.

Tips:

Plan Your Story: Outline the sequence of frames before posting to ensure a coherent narrative.

Use a Beginning, Middle, and End: Start with an introduction, build up the story, and conclude with a clear ending.

Maintain Visual Consistency: Use similar colors, fonts, and styles across frames to create a cohesive look.

Example:

Tell the story of a product launch day, starting with morning preparations, showcasing the event, and ending with a thank-you message to attendees.

Step 5: Showcasing Behind-the-Scenes Content

Why It Matters:

Behind-the-scenes content humanizes your brand and builds a deeper connection with your audience.

Tips:

Daily Operations: Share snippets of your daily operations, such as team meetings or product assembly.

Events: Give a sneak peek into events, from setup to execution.

Team Members: Introduce your team members to personalize your brand.

Processes: Show the process of creating your products or services, highlighting craftsmanship and dedication.

Example:

Film a short clip of your creative team brainstorming ideas for a new campaign, showcasing the collaborative effort involved.

Step 6: Leveraging User-Generated Content

Why It Matters: User-generated content (UGC) boosts credibility and shows appreciation for your audience's contributions.

Tips:

Share Customer Stories: Highlight stories and testimonials from your customers.

Feature User Content: Repost photos and videos from your followers who use your products.

Create a Hashtag Campaign: Encourage your audience to share their content using a branded hashtag.

Example:

Share a story featuring a customer using your product and tag them, thanking them for their support.

Step 7: Analyzing Story Performance

Why It Matters:

Analyzing performance helps you understand what resonates with your audience and refine your strategy.

Tips:

View Insights: Check metrics like views, replies, and interactions to gauge performance.

Identify Patterns: Note which types of stories get the most engagement and replicate successful elements.

Experiment: Try different formats and content types to see what works best.

Example:

If stories featuring behind-the-scenes content get the most views, plan to include more of this type in your future posts.

Step 8: Encouraging Story Interactions

Why It Matters:

Encouraging interactions boosts engagement and makes your stories more memorable.

Tips:

Call to Action: End stories with a call to action, encouraging viewers to swipe up, reply, or participate in a poll.

Engage with Responses: Reply to viewer messages and interactions to build a two-way conversation.

Highlight Interactions: Share some of the responses and interactions in your stories to show appreciation.

Example:

At the end of a story, invite viewers to send in questions for a Q&A session, and feature the best ones in your next story.

Conclusion

Storytelling with Facebook Stories offers a dynamic and personal way to connect with your audience. By creating compelling content, utilizing interactive features, and showcasing behind-the-scenes moments, you can build a deeper connection with your followers.

All Rights Reserved
Morgan Donovan
2024

www.ingramcontent.com/pod-product-compliance
Lightning Source LLC
Chambersburg PA
CBHW050231230526
45470CB00005B/1903